HIROSHIMA AND NAGASAKI

The Atomic Bombings That Shook the World

MICHAEL BURGAN

Consultant:
Richard Bell, PhD
Associate Professor of History
University of Maryland, College Park

CAPSTONE PRESS
a capstone imprint

Tangled History is published by Capstone Press,
1710 Roe Crest Drive, North Mankato, Minnesota 56003
www.capstonepub.com

Library of Congress Cataloging-in-Publication Data
Names: Burgan, Michael, author.
Title: Hiroshima and Nagasaki : the atomic bombings that shook the world /
  by Michael Burgan.
Other titles: Atomic bombings that shook the world
Description: North Mankato, Minnesota : Capstone Press, [2020] | Series:
  Tangled history | Includes bibliographical references and index. |
  Audience: Grades 4–6. | Audience: Ages 8–12.
Identifiers: LCCN 2019006031| ISBN 9781543572568 (hardcover) | ISBN
  9781543575569 (paperback) | ISBN 9781543572605 (eBook pdf)
Subjects: LCSH: Hiroshima-shi (Japan)—History—Bombardment, 1945—
  Juvenile literature. | Nagasaki-shi (Japan)—History—Bombardment,
  1945—Juvenile literature. | Atomic bomb—Blast effect—Juvenile
  literature.
Classification: LCC D767.25.H6 B868 2020 | DDC 940.54/2521954—dc23
LC record available at https://lccn.loc.gov/2019006031

Editorial Credits
Christopher Harbo, editor; Kazuko Collins, designer; Eric Gohl, media
researcher; Laura Manthe, production specialist

Photo Credits
Alamy: Atomic, 4, Science History Images, 22, Sueddeutsche Zeitung Photo, 19,
World History Archive, 48, 52, 55, 80; AP Photo: USAF, 16; Getty Images: Bettmann,
8, FPG, 63, Historical, 68, 89, Jemal Countess, 100, New York Daily News Archive,
29; Library of Congress: cover, 6, 86; National Archives and Records Administration:
27, 38, 50, 60, 71, 90, 95; Newscom: akg-images, 36, 82, Heritage Images/Ann Ronan
Picture Library, 65, Kyodo, 59, MCT/Al Diaz, 76, Photoshot/UPPA, 13, Pictures
From History, 74, World History Archive, 44, ZUMA Press/Mediadrumimage/
Royston Leonard, 78; Shutterstock: Everett Historical, 41; SuperStock: Prisma/
Schultz Reinhard, 93; Wikimedia: Public Domain, 11, 31, 98, 102

Printed and bound in the United States of America.
PA70

TABLE OF CONTENTS

Physicists Albert Einstein (left) and Leo Szilard met in 1939 to write a letter warning President Franklin D. Roosevelt about the dangers of Germany developing an atomic bomb.

FOREWORD

In September 1939, German leader Adolf Hitler sent his troops into Poland, starting World War II (1939–1945) in Europe. Soon his military had taken control of several other countries on the continent, and he was eager to seize more. Hitler thought he had a right to rule over people he considered inferior to him and the members of his Nazi Party.

Even before these invasions, some scientists in the United States worried that Hitler might try to make a new and powerful weapon. The weapon would draw on recent scientific research. By splitting tiny particles called atoms inside the metal uranium, huge amounts of energy could be released. If that process was carefully controlled, it could be developed into a bomb that could kill tens of thousands of people instantly. The explosion would also release large amounts of radiation, a form of energy that is harmful in high doses.

Physicists Albert Einstein and Leo Szilard told President Franklin D. Roosevelt about the possibility of this new weapon. They said Germany could develop one. They told the president he should consider building such a bomb too.

The United States was not at war when Roosevelt learned about this potential new weapon. But he told some U.S. government officials to study the idea of building what came to be called an atomic bomb. The British, who were fighting the Germans, were also researching such a bomb, and they shared information with the United States. Soon the two countries were working together on an atomic bomb.

Smoke billowed from the USS *West Virginia* after it was struck by torpedoes and bombs during Japan's surprise attack on Pearl Harbor.

The work on the atomic bomb became more urgent after December 7, 1941, when Japan attacked the U.S. naval base at Pearl Harbor on the island of Oahu, in Hawaii. Together with Germany and Italy, Japan was part of the Axis powers. Right after the attack, the United States declared war on Japan. But soon thereafter it joined the other nations of the Allied forces, including Great Britain and the Soviet Union, by declaring war on Germany and Italy as well.

During the summer of 1942, the British and U.S. effort to build an atomic bomb was named the

Manhattan Project. Some of the early work took place in Manhattan, a part of New York City, and other important research went on in Chicago. But starting in February 1943, the focus of the major Allied research switched to a remote spot in the mountains northwest of Santa Fe, New Mexico. The scientist J. Robert Oppenheimer was chosen to head the Manhattan Project at the newly built Los Alamos Scientific Laboratory. Oppenheimer's task was to design and build a workable atomic bomb as quickly as possible.

Oppenheimer recruited scientists from around the country. By July 1945, the United States was ready to test its first atomic bomb. President Roosevelt had died that April, and Vice President Harry Truman became president. Germany surrendered in May, so Truman knew that if the United States dropped one of the bombs, the target would be somewhere in Japan. He, his generals, and the scientists in the Manhattan Project anxiously waited to hear how the atomic test would turn out. If it went well, Truman would have to decide whether to use the bomb on Japan.

1

Luis Alvarez works with a Geiger counter, which is used to measure radioactivity, in his laboratory.

THE BOMB WORKS

Luis Alvarez kneeled on the floor of the B-29 bomber. On either side of him were the plane's pilot and copilot. Alvarez's assistant, Lawrence Johnston, and several other scientists sat in the rear of the plane. Along with Alvarez, their mission was to observe the first explosion of an atomic bomb and measure the effects of the blast.

As a physicist, Alvarez had known about the effort to build the bomb even before the United States had entered the war. Then, after the Japanese bombing of Pearl Harbor, he had worked in both Chicago and Los Alamos on the Manhattan Project.

Alvarez helped design detonators. He focused on the implosion method of triggering an atomic blast. This method used plutonium, a radioactive material created when uranium is bombarded with particles called neutrons. These particles are found in the center of atoms. In the bomb, powerful explosives crushed a piece of plutonium, causing an implosion. The implosion then released the energy inside the plutonium.

The Manhattan Project scientists also created a bomb with a different type of detonator. This bomb used a gun-like device to fire one piece of uranium at another. The collision of the two pieces of uranium at high speeds started the process that unleashed the bomb's explosive power.

By early 1945, the scientists in Los Alamos believed they had successfully designed a working bomb. Alvarez had volunteered to go along on any real bombing missions so he could see and measure the effects of the blast. First, though, the scientist would witness the test explosion about to take place.

The B-29 carrying Alvarez and the others circled at 24,000 feet above the test site in the desert. The plane was 25 miles away from a spot given the nickname "Trinity." The bomb waiting to explode there was called "Gadget." It used the implosion detonator that Alvarez and others had worked hard to perfect.

As dawn broke, clouds filled the sky and Alvarez could not see Trinity's initial explosion. Then, at 5:30 a.m., he looked out the tiny window on Captain William "Deak" Parsons's side of the plane. Alvarez saw intense light fill the sky, followed by a ball of fire with a reddish-orange glow. Then a huge, mushroom-shaped cloud from the blast rose into the air. Alvarez guessed that it was 40,000 feet high. Parsons and the others on board soon felt a bump as a wave of energy from the bomb shook the plane. Alvarez did not feel the jolt. But he knew that the bomb had worked.

A bright, reddish-orange mushroom cloud rose thousands of feet above the Trinity test site moments after Gadget was detonated.

President Harry Truman

President Harry Truman sat in his room writing letters, telling his wife and sister about his first experiences in Potsdam, Germany. He had arrived there several days before to meet with British Prime Minister Winston Churchill and Joseph Stalin, the leader of the Soviet Union. Those two Allied leaders had met several times before with President Roosevelt, but they had just held their first meeting with Truman the day before. The three men wanted to discuss the situation in Europe after Germany's surrender and the ongoing war with Japan.

The testing of the atomic bomb in New Mexico was also on Truman's mind. Since taking office in April, his top aides had told him about the bomb's power—assuming it worked as the scientists said it would. They also discussed with him how he might use the bomb.

President Harry Truman (center) met with British Prime Minister Winston Churchill (left) and Soviet leader Joseph Stalin (right) at the Potsdam Conference to discuss postwar Europe and how to get Japan to surrender.

Some advisors suggested he drop the bomb in a remote area to show the Japanese its destructive power. Others wanted Truman to use it without warning on a city where the Japanese built weapons and supplies for their troops. But most of the advisors were convinced Truman had to use the bomb. The shock value of it, one had told him, would help end the war. And if the war against Japan dragged on, the United States would likely have to launch an invasion of Japan. That would lead to the deaths of tens of thousands of U.S. troops.

Truman was starting to think he would drop the bomb—if it worked—when Secretary of War Henry Stimson came to see him. Stimson relayed a coded message: "The little boy is as husky as his big brother." Stimson explained that the message meant the atomic bomb had worked.

A few days later, Stimson returned to Truman's room in Potsdam with a more detailed report about the test. The bomb had exploded with the force of up to 20,000 tons of TNT. The light from the blast could be seen for up to 180 miles, and the explosion had created a crater 1,000 feet wide.

Truman was pleased with the report. He did not necessarily like having control over such a powerful weapon. But using it, he hoped, would finally end World War II.

Sergeant George "Bob" Caron

Tinian island, Pacific Ocean,
July 24, 1945

After training for months, Sergeant Bob Caron was eager to get back in the air—even for only a test flight. Caron was a tail gunner on a B-29 bomber. But the ones he and other members of the 393rd Bomb Squadron flew were not typical B-29s. They were specially made to carry one large, heavy bomb. The men and the planes were part of a secret mission to drop a new weapon. Some of the men stationed with Caron on the Pacific island of Tinian called it the "gimmick."

In July, Caron and other members of his crew started flying test bombing runs over Japan. Their B-29 carried a single 5-ton bomb painted orange. The men had dropped similar bombs on test runs

Sergeant George "Bob" Caron

over the desert in the United States. The crew called these bombs "pumpkins."

Today Caron and the crew were carrying a pumpkin to drop over the city of Kobe, Japan. The B-29 could fly above the range of most Japanese guns, but that did not stop the enemy from firing at them. In his turret at the back of the plane, Caron watched the burst of the guns' shells. He counted the number of explosions to try to figure out how many guns the Japanese had. That information could be useful to the pilot if they flew again in this area. Caron never knew where his next mission would be. But all the men in the squadron would be ready when the day to drop the gimmick came.

President Harry Truman

Potsdam, Germany,
July 25, 1945

With another day in Potsdam done, President Truman sat down to write in his diary. After his meeting with Secretary Stimson the day before, Truman had also met with Winston Churchill and

U.S. and British military advisors. They had decided to use the bomb within several weeks.

On this day, the order went out authorizing the use of the bomb. And now Truman wrote in his diary, "We have discovered the most terrible bomb in the history of the world." He explained his decision not to bomb Tokyo, the capital, or the old capital city of Kyoto. "The target will be a purely military one," he went on. He was glad that Germany's former leader, Adolf Hitler, had not been able to develop an atomic bomb. And Truman noted that even if the bomb is terrible, "it can be made most useful."

Foreign Minister Shigenori Togo

Tokyo, Japan,
July 28, 1945

As he read the news and messages from Japanese diplomats, Foreign Minister Shigenori Togo wondered how the war would end. He knew it would end soon because Japan could not keep fighting much longer.

Japanese Foreign Minister Shigenori Togo

As the government's top advisor on foreign relations, Togo had opposed the war from the start. But in 1941, generals and politicians who wanted to fight the United States and Great Britain had persuaded Japan's ruler, Emperor Hirohito, to attack. Some wanted to keep fighting now, while Togo was eager to end the war.

Now Togo was going over the reports coming out of Potsdam, Germany. The United States, Great Britain, and China had just demanded that Japan surrender without conditions. In the so-called Potsdam Declaration, Togo read that, without complete surrender, "the alternative for Japan is prompt and utter destruction." But Japan's prime minister, Kantaro Suzuki, had only the day before told Japanese reporters that the country would ignore the Allies's demand.

The other major Allied nation at the Potsdam Conference, the Soviet Union, had not signed the declaration. Togo had been working for several weeks with Naotake Sato, his ambassador in the Soviet capital of Moscow. The two diplomats hoped they could convince Soviet leader Joseph Stalin to work out a peace deal between the two sides. At the very least, they wanted to keep the Soviet Union from entering the war against Japan.

Togo sent Sato a message. He worried that the Russians might have shared some of Japan's earlier messages to them with the other Allies. He expressed his concern about "what attitude the Russians will take toward Japan in the future."

Two days later, Sato wrote back to Togo. Sato told the foreign minister he believed that, without unconditional surrender, the Soviet Union would enter the war against Japan. But Togo knew the supporters of the war would reject surrendering with those terms. And Japan would continue to suffer as the United States carried out deadly bombing raids across the country.

2

Corporal Abe Spitzer (front row, second from right) with his B-29 bomber crew, including pilot Major Charles Sweeney (top row, far right)

HEADING TO HIROSHIMA

Abe Spitzer joined the other men of the 393rd Bomb Squadron as they filed into a conference room. An armed guard checked off each man's name as he entered. Spitzer smiled when Ray Gallagher joked to the guard, "We're on your side. Remember?" The guard did not smile back.

Spitzer was the radio operator on one of the B-29s that had been flying practice bombing raids over Japan. He and the rest of the men were going to learn more about their next mission from Captain Parsons. Everyone in the room knew the 393rd was going to drop some new kind of bomb. But now Parsons gave them more details.

"We think it will wipe out almost everything within a three-mile area," Parsons said. "One single solitary bomb will do all that."

Parsons went on to describe the test explosion that had taken place several weeks before in New Mexico. One of the flight crews in the room would have the job of dropping one, or maybe more, of these bombs from a B-29.

The meeting went on for several hours. The other speakers included Colonel Paul Tibbets. He had already been chosen to pilot the plane that would drop the first bomb. He told the men that the bomb would help shorten the war by at least six months.

Spitzer learned that his plane would be one of three to fly on the first bombing mission. The plane was called The Great Artiste, and its pilot was Major Charles Sweeney. Along with its crew, the plane would carry scientists who would observe and measure the blast. The third plane on the mission would carry a photographer. Before these planes took off, three other planes would fly ahead to check the weather conditions over three possible targets. Those conditions would help determine which city to bomb.

As Spitzer heard all the details, he began to sweat. The bombers would fly alone. No U.S. fighter planes would be there to protect them if the Japanese sent up their own planes to attack. And as the radio operator, he would have to listen for the messages from the airfield that instructed The Great Artiste on what to do. Spitzer began to question why he had taken this job.

Why hadn't I stayed on the ground? he thought.

As the meeting was about to end, a naval officer told the flight crews they would be famous. "We'll be famous," someone behind Spitzer called out, "if we live."

Hideko Tamura

Kimita, Japan,
August 4, 1945

Hideko Tamura looked down the steps outside her school and saw her mother approaching. Tamura ran down to hug her—their first hug in almost four months.

In April, 10-year-old Tamura had joined other elementary school students from Hiroshima in the village of Kimita. They had been sent out of the city to protect them from enemy bombing raids. But conditions at the school were poor, and Tamura had developed health problems. She had written to her mother and begged her to come now. On this day, Tamura got her wish.

Mrs. Tamura was glad to see her daughter, but she wanted her to stay in Kimita one more full day. She thought it would be good for her to rest before returning to Hiroshima. But Tamura begged her mother to go home as soon as possible.

Finally Mrs. Tamura agreed. The next day they would return to Hiroshima.

President Harry Truman

At sea on the USS *Augusta*,
August 4, 1945

As he sailed back to the United States from Europe, all President Truman could do was wait. He had made the decision to drop the atomic bomb, and now his generals would decide which target to hit and when.

The day before on the *Augusta*, Truman had sat down with several reporters to tell them about the bomb. His mixed feelings about the new weapon

President Truman's decision to use the atomic bomb was not an easy one, but he believed it was the only way to end the war quickly.

had come through. But today he felt relaxed as he waited to hear what would happen when it was finally dropped on Japan.

Foreign Minister Shigenori Togo

Tokyo, Japan,
August 4, 1945

Foreign Minister Togo read Ambassador Sato's most recent message. They had been in almost constant communication for several days. Togo still hoped that the Soviet Union could play a role in ending the war. But in Moscow, Sato was getting frustrated. Togo had not said exactly what Japan wanted for it to surrender, and Sato doubted the Russians would act anyway. In this latest message, Sato said time was running out for the Japanese to make a plan for ending the war. Otherwise, Sato feared, "All Japan will be reduced to ashes."

Sergeant Bob Caron

Tinian island, Pacific Ocean,
August 5, 1945

Sergeant Caron was playing softball with some of the other crewmen when he got the word to meet with Colonel Tibbets and Captain Robert Lewis. Caron had flown with Lewis before on B-29 number 82. Now Lewis would be Tibbets's copilot on that plane on the mission to drop the gimmick, and Caron would remain part of the crew as the tail gunner. Their plane was now called the Enola Gay, named for Tibbets's mother. The bomb they would carry was nicknamed "Little Boy."

Caron left his softball game and joined Tibbets, Lewis, and the other officers who would be flying on the Enola Gay. Altogether the plane would carry 12 men. A photographer was there too, and he grouped the men together to take an official picture.

That evening, Caron lay on his bed and thought about his wife, Kay, back home in Monarch Pass, Colorado. He and Kay had recently had a baby. The hours passed quickly, and just before midnight he went with the other crew members for one last briefing session.

Sergeant Bob Caron (far right) and the crew of the B-29 bomber, the Enola Gay

Corporal Abe Spitzer

Corporal Spitzer woke up and looked at the clock. He had been having trouble sleeping the past two nights, so he had taken a nap. Now he had slept through dinner. He got up and got ready for the last briefing before the B-29s took off for Japan.

At the briefing, officers gave more details about the mission. The primary target was Hiroshima, a city of about 318,000 people. In it was a supply base for the Japanese military, thousands of soldiers, and factories that made weapons. An intelligence officer stressed to the pilots that after dropping the bomb, "Get the hell away fast. You can't tell what will happen. Just get the hell away as quick as you can."

Spitzer returned to the barracks with the other men in his crew. Even though they would take off in just a few hours, he felt relaxed. The men talked about what they would do after the war, and they made plans to get together when they were back in the United States.

Luis Alvarez

Luis Alvarez pulled on his flight suit. He and his assistant, Lawrence Johnston, had just left the last briefing before the bombing mission. During the briefing, Alvarez had learned that the bomb, Little Boy, weighed almost 10,000 pounds and used the gun system detonator, rather than the implosion method he had developed. He also heard

Luis Alvarez donned protective flight gear for his mission aboard The Great Artiste, which was to measure the power of the atomic blast over Hiroshima, Japan.

Colonel Tibbets say the bomb would be as powerful as 20,000 tons of TNT. But Alvarez knew his job would be to take measurements and record a more precise size of the blast.

Alvarez and Johnston walked out to the runway. It was lit up with powerful lights so cameras could record the historic moment. The men boarded The Great Artiste and strapped themselves into their seats. At 2:47 a.m., the plane began to roll down the runway, following the Enola Gay.

Soon the plane was airborne. And though he had work to do, Alvarez could not fight off the urge to sleep. He felt relaxed, not tense, as he prepared to take part in this historic mission.

Sergeant Bob Caron

Over the Pacific Ocean,
August 6, 1945

During the takeoff, Sergeant Caron sat wedged in his gun turret. He had been told it was safer there if the plane had any problems and crashed into the ocean. But this takeoff was smooth. Once the plane was in the air, he moved into the center part of the plane to talk to some of the other crew. After a while, Colonel Tibbets came back to join them. He looked at Caron.

"Bob, have you figured out what we're doing this morning?" Tibbets asked. "You can guess whatever you want."

Caron thought back to a physics book he had read when he was still training in the United States. "Colonel, are we splitting atoms this morning?" he replied.

Tibbets gave Caron a funny look, as if he was not expecting him to say that. "Yes," the colonel confirmed.

Soon after, Tibbets went on the intercom and told the whole crew that they were carrying the world's first atomic bomb into battle.

Hideko Tamura

Hiroshima, Japan,
August 6, 1945

The sun was shining when Hideko Tamura woke up in her own bed for the first time in months. Her mother had prepared rice porridge for breakfast.

She had made something soft because she knew Hideko had a toothache. Then her mother prepared to leave for the day to work for the government.

"See you just in a short time," her mother called as she headed out.

At 7:15 a.m., Tamura heard air-raid sirens go off in the neighborhood. Across Japan the sirens were often followed by enemy bomber planes. Tamura turned on the radio and heard that three U.S. planes were heading toward Hiroshima. She was not worried—how much damage could three planes do? But if they attacked, she knew to run to the concrete bomb shelter in the backyard. Everyone in the city had gone through drills to prepare for an attack.

After listening to the radio for 15 minutes, Tamura heard that the planes had turned around. She ran through the house. "The warning is off, everybody, the warning is off," she shouted to her family.

"We didn't pay much attention, Hideko, it's so nice out," her aunt called out.

Tamura turned off the radio and began to read a book.

Corporal Abe Spitzer

It was just after 8 a.m. on Corporal Spitzer's watch and an hour earlier in Japan. Soon the reports from the three weather planes would go back to the base at Tinian, and then he would receive their report. He watched the minutes tick by. There was still no report. *Had he missed it somehow?* Spitzer wondered. *Was there something wrong with the radio?* Then, finally, the radio began to make a noise. Spitzer reached for a pencil, but he was so nervous his hand was shaking and he dropped it. He reached for another pencil. This time his hand was steady. He listened to the coded message and wrote down what it meant: "Target clear . . . Visibility unlimited." That meant the attack on the primary target was on. The bomb the Enola Gay was carrying would soon be dropped over Hiroshima.

3

The Little Boy atomic bomb sat on a platform before being loaded into the Enola Gay.

LITTLE BOY FALLS

The Enola Gay was now just minutes away from its target. Back in his gun turret, Sergeant Caron scanned the skies for any sign of enemy planes or antiaircraft fire. There were none. Then he heard a signal sent by Major Thomas Ferebee. That meant just 15 seconds to go before the bomb would be released and sail down some 31,000 feet.

Caron could tell when Little Boy began to fall. The sudden release of 5 tons of weight made the plane rise a bit. Then Colonel Tibbets made a hard right turn to escape the effects of the blast.

As the plane straightened out, the pilot called back to Caron, "Bob, let me know what you see when you see something." Since the plane was flying away from Hiroshima and Caron was in the rear, he would have the best view of the blast. Like the others on board, Caron wore special goggles meant to protect his eyes from blinding light.

As the Enola Gay continued to speed away, Caron saw the bright flash from the exploding Little Boy, and then he watched a ring rising up from the ground. He did not know what it was, but the ring soon rose up to the Enola Gay and jolted it. After a few seconds, Colonel Tibbets called over the intercom, "Do you see anything yet?"

"Nothing yet, colonel," Caron replied. But almost as soon as he said it, he saw a huge, mushroom-shaped cloud rise into the air. It was white on the outside and bright red in its center. The third plane on the mission, Necessary Evil, carried a camera crew, but Caron had a camera, too, and he began

Seen from the air, Little Boy's atomic blast raced outward and upward, forming a giant mushroom cloud high above Hiroshima, Japan.

photographing the growing cloud. He knew they were flying at 31,000 feet. Caron guessed that the mushroom cloud eventually reached 50,000 feet.

As the Enola Gay continued to pull away from Hiroshima, Caron looked down on the city. What looked like a bubbling wave of molasses was spreading out, and fires were everywhere. Even when the plane was nearly 300 miles away from Hiroshima, Caron could still see the atomic cloud in the sky.

Dr. Michihiko Hachiya

Hiroshima, Japan,
August 6, 1945, 8:16 a.m.

Dr. Michihiko Hachiya lay on the floor of his living room. It was 8:16 a.m., and he was exhausted after spending the night at his hospital. Suddenly he saw a brilliant flash of light outside, followed by another. Then he noticed that the roof of his house was sagging. He struggled to get up and run outside, but parts of the house had already collapsed and blocked his way. As he finally managed to get outside, he realized he was naked. What had happened to his clothes? Then he noticed cuts over one side of his body. A large splinter of wood was stuck in his leg and his cheek was torn. Blood was everywhere.

"Where are you?" Hachiya called out to his wife, Yaeko. She soon joined him outside, her clothes torn and covered with blood.

"We'll be all right," he said to her. "Only let's get out of here as fast as we can."

The two ran through the street. They stumbled at times and finally tripped over something and fell. As he got up, Hachiya looked down and realized he had tripped over someone. Hachiya saw it was a soldier, and he apologized to him. But the soldier did not respond. The doctor now realized the man was dead, crushed by a huge gate that had fallen into the street.

Tsutomu Yamaguchi

Hiroshima, Japan,
August 6, 1945, 8:16 a.m.

Tsutomu Yamaguchi walked through a field several miles from the center of Hiroshima. The 29-year-old engineer was visiting the city on business. Today was supposed to be his last day here. Then he could return to his home in Nagasaki, some 190 miles away. He got off the trolley that had taken him partway into town. On one side of the street was a field of sweet potatoes. Yamaguchi noticed the dew on the potatoes glistening in the sun.

As he walked, Yamaguchi heard a plane in the distance—an enemy bomber. He looked up and saw two tiny white parachutes fluttering down to

Seen from the ground, the atomic blast over Hiroshima towered thousands of feet above the Japanese countryside.

the ground. Then he saw a bright flash. Without thinking, he followed the training he had learned in the navy. He fell to the ground, rolled into a nearby ditch in the sweet potato field, and plugged his ears with his thumbs. If a bomb went off nearby, he hoped he could save his hearing.

Even with his ears plugged, Yamaguchi heard an incredibly loud explosion. The ground began to shake and then snap—the way someone might crack a whip. The earth's movement launched him 3 feet into the air. Falling back to the ground, he looked up and saw a huge ball of fire erupting over the center of Hiroshima. Back in the ditch, Yamaguchi looked around and saw burning pieces of paper and clothing falling through the air. He noticed that the left side of his body was hot. The skin on his left arm had been burned black. His face, too, had been affected by the blast, and he put mud on it to try to cool it. As he looked around and saw destruction all around him, Yamaguchi realized he had to get back to Nagasaki as soon as he could to be with his wife and son.

Hideko Tamura

Hideko Tamura was still reading when she noticed a huge flash outside her window. That flash was followed by an enormous explosion that shook the walls of her house. She stood up but was battered by objects falling off walls and shelves. The wind picked up and blew dust through the house.

Then, as suddenly as all the noise and movement and wind had begun, it stopped. Tamura was covered with dirt and debris, but she had survived whatever had just happened. Still, she knew the danger was not over. She remembered what her mother had told her to do if bombs ever fell on Hiroshima, "Leave immediately before the fires surround you." Tamura knew that during U.S. bombing raids in Tokyo earlier that year, huge fires had caused incredible damage.

Tamura called out for her grandmother and other relatives who lived in the home. The women had some minor injuries, but then Tamura heard her Uncle Hisao.

"Where are you?" he called from the backyard. "Isn't anyone alive?"

The women rushed out back and saw Hisao sitting on the ground, covered with blood. Large pieces of glass jutted out of his body, as if someone had stabbed him with them.

"The end has come, this is the end, we are finished," he moaned.

Tamura now realized that she was bleeding, too, after getting some glass in the bottom of her right foot. She removed the glass, wrapped her foot, then ran over to her family. She repeated her

Survivors of the initial atomic blast ran for their lives as raging fires swept through Hiroshima.

mother's instructions to flee immediately before fires started blocking the streets. But her relatives were too shocked to move. Tamura ran out of the yard by herself, calling back to them, "You've got to leave! You've got to get away!"

Out on the street, Tamura realized that a bomb had not only gone off in her neighborhood. Buildings all around had been destroyed, and injured people staggered through the streets. As the wind picked up, she saw small flames quickly grow into bigger fires.

Once again, Tamura remembered her mother's words, "Go to the water, child, stay close to the river, save yourself from fire." Limping as fast as she could, Tamura headed for the Ota River.

Luis Alvarez

Over the Pacific Ocean,
August 6, 1945, 8:16 a.m.

Flying over Japan, Luis Alvarez was focused on his scientific equipment. Once Little Boy was released, Major Sweeney swung The Great Artiste around. This time, unlike at the New Mexico test bombing, Alvarez felt a wave of energy from the blast rock the plane. Then he went to one of the aircraft's windows and looked out to see the cloud rising over Hiroshima.

As The Great Artiste flew back to Tinian, Alvarez wrote a letter to his four-year-old son, Walter. Alvarez knew the boy would not understand much of it now, but he would when he was older. And, of course, by the time the letter reached the United States, the whole world would know about the dropping of the first atomic bomb.

But now Alvarez wrote, "Only the crews of our three B-29s, and the unfortunate residents of the Hiroshima district in Japan are aware of what has happened to aerial warfare. . . . A single plane, disguised as a friendly transport, can now wipe out an entire city."

President Harry Truman

At sea on the USS *Augusta*,
August 6, 1945, 12 p.m.

President Truman sat down to lunch with some of the sailors on the ship. One of the officers came over with a message from Secretary of War Henry

Stimson. Truman read that the atomic bomb had been dropped on Hiroshima. "Results clear-cut successful in all respects."

Truman grabbed the officer's hand and said, "This is the greatest thing in history." After a few minutes, the president stood up and announced to all the sailors, "We have just dropped a new bomb on Japan which has more power than 20,000 tons of TNT. It has been an overwhelming success!" Truman smiled as the sailors around him began to cheer.

A little later, the sailors gathered to hear the broadcast of a message Truman had written earlier. It was to be released after the dropping of the bomb. Across the United States, people heard the same message on their radios. The president had written that if Japan did not accept the Allies's terms for surrender, the Japanese could expect "a rain of ruin from the air, the like of which has never been seen on this earth."

After the atomic bombing, survivors combed through the tangled debris and skeletal ruins of Hiroshima.

A DEADLY DAY

Dr. Michihiko Hachiya

Hiroshima, Japan,
August 6, 1945

Dr. Hachiya did not live far from the hospital where he worked, so he and his wife, Yaeko, began to walk there. Hachiya collapsed in the street, got up, and continued. For a time he had forgotten he was naked, but now Yaeko gave him her apron to put around his body. After a bit, Hachiya fell again.

"Go without me," he told his wife. "Bring someone to help."

After Yaeko left, Hachiya managed to walk a little farther on his own. His spirits lifted when he saw the hospital up ahead. Then he noticed people walking down the streets in a funny way. They held their arms away from their sides. Hachiya realized their arms were badly burned, and the people did not want to brush them against their bodies.

Hachiya finally reached the hospital and saw the welcoming faces of many of the people he worked with. They made him lie down on a stretcher and began to treat his wounds. As they did, Hachiya looked out the window.

"Fire!" he shouted. "The hospital is on fire!"

Doctors and nurses ordered everyone to leave and went to rescue the patients. Two people picked up Hachiya's stretcher and brought him outside. As the fire spread, several of his friends moved him again.

The atomic bomb obliterated Hiroshima, leaving behind nothing more than crumbling foundations and charred trees.

As the fire inched closer, someone took Hachiya off the stretcher and pulled him along. Hachiya lost consciousness. The next thing he knew, an old woman who worked at the hospital called out, "Cheer up, doctor! Everything will be all right. We have nothing further to fear from the fire."

Hachiya looked over. The fire was out. The second floor was badly burned, but the first floor had been saved. His friends carried him back into the hospital, and one of the doctors stitched up the many wounds that covered his body.

Tsutomo Yamaguchi

Hiroshima, Japan,
August 6, 1945

As his initial shock after the blast passed, Tsutomo Yamaguchi felt the pain from burns on his neck and arms. He was desperate for a drink of water, and he took some from a nearby river. He tried to eat a small biscuit he had in his pocket, but he immediately threw up. When he tried to drink more water later, he could not keep that down either.

Yamaguchi decided to head to the manufacturing plant where he had been working as a ship designer. When he reached it, he saw that the blast had destroyed some buildings. Workers were gathered

Buildings caved in on themselves when the atomic blast swept across Hiroshima's landscape.

outside the plant. A first-aid station had been set up, and a security guard told Yamaguchi to put an ointment on his burns.

"We should go back to the dorm," one of

Yamaguchi's friends from the plant said. Hiroshima sat on a bay, and different channels of the Ota River cut through the city. The plant was on the water, as was the factory dorm. Yamaguchi and others took a boat to Uzina Harbor and then began walking to the dorm. They saw the reflection of flames from the burning city in the water.

At the dorm, Yamaguchi saw that some of the building had been destroyed. Everyone there agreed that the women and children would sleep in the shelters that were still standing. The men, meanwhile, would take turns sleeping outside, making sure that none of the fires in the city spread near them.

Hideko Tamura

Hiroshima, Japan,
August 6, 1945

Hideko Tamura joined a mass of survivors heading toward the Ota River. She wondered if her mother and father were all right. "Please, God, keep them safe," she prayed. She remembered her mother had told her that if anything bad happened in Hiroshima, they would meet in a village in the country called Tomo. Tamura knew she had to try to get there. Then she heard a voice call her name. She turned and saw one of her young neighbors, a girl named Noriko.

"What happened to you?" Tamura asked the wounded girl.

"There was this flash, and it burned me," Noriko said. Tamura could see that her skin was red, and blisters covered part of her face.

Surrounded by death and destruction, some children in Hiroshima gathered together for support in the aftermath of the atomic bombing.

"Yes, I saw the flash," Tamura said. As she spoke, she saw Noriko's face begin to swell. Noriko was with some of her classmates along the river, and Tamura joined them. As they walked, Tamura saw more children who were badly burned, some with skin hanging off their arms.

Tamura's foot began to bleed again, and she washed it off in the river. She hobbled along with Noriko until they saw a truck come along the river. The driver offered rides to anyone who wanted them. As a crowd of people rushed toward the truck, Tamura tried to keep up with them. When she reached it, the driver said it was full.

Tamura pointed to her injured foot and said she could not walk any farther. She begged the man to let her in. Finally he agreed.

After a 30-minute drive, the truck let them off at a small hospital outside the city. Tamura asked if someone could treat her foot. A man told her they were only taking care of serious burn victims. Tamura asked if he knew where the village of Tomo was. He said yes, but he was too busy to help. He told Tamura to ask someone else.

Tamura began to walk, hoping she would find someone who could guide her to Tomo.

Corporal Abe Spitzer

Corporal Spitzer was exhausted when The Great Artiste and the two other planes touched down in Tinian. Stepping off the plane, he saw more of the bright lights that had covered the airfield before they had taken off for Japan. Now the photographers and filmmakers wanted to capture the airmen as they returned from their historic mission. Many high-ranking officers were there, too, and one of them pinned a metal on Colonel Tibbets.

Soon Spitzer and the others were brought into a room and questioned about what had happened. Spitzer did not say much. At one point someone asked him, "What was it like?"

"It was hell. Absolute hell."

What Spitzer thought, but did not say, was that with the dropping of the atomic bomb, they had learned how to kill too many people too quickly.

Dr. Takashi Nagai

Nagasaki, Japan,
August 6, 1945

By the end of the day, the first reports of
a terrible bombing in Hiroshima had reached
Dr. Takashi Nagai in Nagasaki. Nagai told
his wife, Midori, that it was time to send their
children to the country to stay with their
grandmother. They would be safer there.

Nagai, though, was not ready to leave
Nagasaki. As a doctor and teacher, he still had
work to do. But he also knew that he would
not be on the job for long because he was dying
of cancer.

The end would come for him soon, whether
by bombs or his disease. But he had to protect
his children. Especially as he remembered the
pamphlet the U.S. planes had recently dropped
over Nagasaki. Japanese government officials had
told the people not to read the pamphlets, saying
the Americans were just spreading lies. But Nagai
had read one, and its message had frightened him.

It said, "In April Nagasaki was all flowers. In August it will be flame showers."

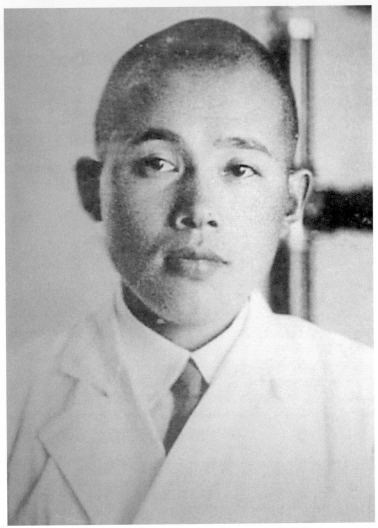

Dr. Takashi Nagai

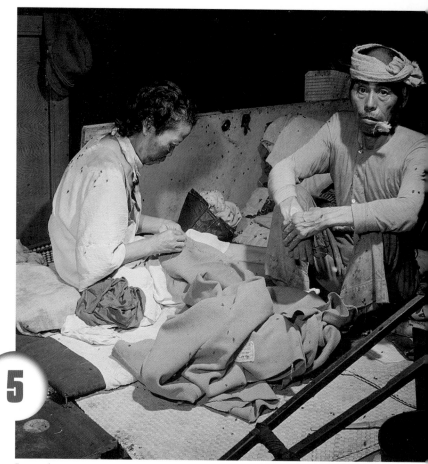

Injured survivors of the Hiroshima bombing sought shelter wherever they could find it, including this fly-infested hospital set up in a bank building.

STAYING ALIVE

Hideko Tamura

Hideko Tamura huddled in a small room in the house of a wealthy farmer in Kabe. The day before, she had been lucky to find someone to help her. A man on a bicycle had stopped to talk to her. He invited her to his home, and she ate with his family. They let her stay the night, too, and this morning the man had ridden to Hiroshima to try to find her family. Amazingly he found them, and almost everyone was alive. But Tamura's heart sank when she learned her mother was missing.

Now Tamura and her family were together in Kabe. Her Uncle Hisao had bandages on his body where a doctor had removed pieces of glass. Some pieces were still inside him. Tamura's grandmother and Aunt Kiyoko had bruises, but they were not badly hurt. Tamura learned that one of her cousins was missing as well. Her uncle said that tomorrow they would all return to Hiroshima to look for him and her mother.

Tamura nodded. She could not bear to think that her mother was lying somewhere in pain, or even dead.

Foreign Minister Shigenori Togo

Tokyo, Japan,
August 7, 1945

Foreign Minister Togo was meeting with Japanese military and government officials to discuss what Japan should do. Reports of the devastation in Hiroshima had begun reaching them the day before. But only this morning did they learn that almost the entire city had been destroyed by a single bomb.

An aide also alerted Togo to a radio message President Harry Truman had made. The president said that the United States had dropped an atomic bomb on Hiroshima. He also said it would drop

Foreign Minister Shigenori Togo (back row, second from left) stood for a photo with Japanese Prime Minister Hideki Tojo (front row, center) and his cabinet members in 1943.

more bombs if Japan did not accept the conditions for surrender outlined in the Potsdam Declaration. Now Togo and Japanese military and government officials were meeting to discuss what to do.

Togo said the government should consider surrendering, since the United States seemed to have more atomic bombs.

Several army generals disagreed. They said Japan did not know for sure that the United States had dropped an atomic bomb or how bad the damage was in Hiroshima.

Togo realized that the military leaders were still not ready to admit defeat. But later that day, he met with Army Minister General Korechika Anami. The general said he was ready to fight on, but he admitted that Japan would lose the war in the end.

Togo said it was now up to the emperor to decide what Japan should do next.

Dr. Michihiko Hachiya

Hiroshima, Japan,
August 7, 1945

After sleeping through the night, Dr. Hachiya woke up to screams of pain from some of the injured who filled the hospital. Soon one of his coworkers, Dr. Hanaoka, came to see him.

"Dr. Hachiya, you don't know how happy I am to see you!" Hanaoka said. "After seeing what has happened to Hiroshima, it's a miracle anyone survived."

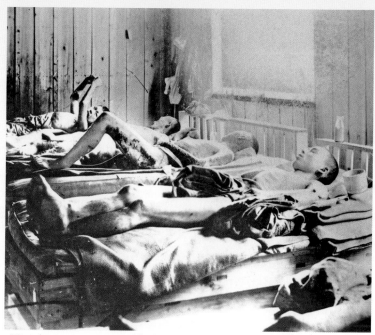

Hiroshima survivors quickly filled whole rooms lined with beds as they suffered the effects of radiation burns all over their bodies.

Hachiya replied that it was good to see him. Then he asked, "Where have you been, and how did you get here?"

Hanaoka told Hachiya that he had just come from another hospital, located more than half a mile from where the bomb exploded. Everything between the bomb site and the hospital and been destroyed. Inside streetcars, Hanaoka said, were "dozens of bodies, blackened beyond recognition."

He described seeing reservoirs filled with dead bodies. At the hospital he had just left, Hanaoka said, "It is swamped with patients, and outside the dead and dying are lined up on either side of the street."

Other doctors came to Hachiya and told him similar tales, filled with death and destruction. And Hachiya heard that some patients coming to the hospital were vomiting and suffering from diarrhea. He wondered if some kind of poison gas or harmful germs had been released when the bomb exploded.

Tsutomo Yamaguchi

Hiroshima, Japan,
August 7, 1945

Tsutomo Yamaguchi woke up and saw that the fires had not spread any closer during the night. He went into one of the dorms to get food, then began walking to the train station. Throughout the city, he saw the remains of buildings still smoking from the fires. As he went, Yamaguchi sometimes walked into dead bodies lying on the sidewalk. Some of the bodies were burned badly, and Yamaguchi grew weak in the knees as he passed by them.

Finally, around 1 p.m., he reached the station. Despite the bombing, a train was still running to Nagasaki. Yamaguchi boarded it thinking that he would soon see his wife and son again, and he would be safe.

Hideko Tamura

Hiroshima, Japan,
August 8, 1945

Along with her family, Hideko Tamura walked to different first-aid stations across Hiroshima, hoping to find her mother and cousin. At one station she recognized a young woman who taught at her school. She was curled up under a small blue blanket.

"Are you all right?" Tamura asked.

"It's so hard . . . it's so hard," the young woman said, her voice soft. The woman's body began to shake violently, then stopped. Tamura was terrified as she realized the woman had died right in front of her.

Survivors poured into relief stations that were set up to treat cuts, burns, and other injuries caused by the atomic bombing.

The Tamura family moved on to a Buddhist temple, where many of the injured were gathered. Hideko called out, "Is Mrs. Kimiko Tamura here? Please answer me, please." But her mother did not call out. All Hideko heard were the cries of people desperate for water.

Her aunt and uncle did not have any luck finding Hideko's cousin, either. They heard tales from the parents of some of her cousin's classmates. Most of the students were either dead or missing. Hideko did not know if she would ever see her cousin or her mother again.

Foreign Minister Shigenori Togo

Tokyo, Japan,
August 8, 1945

Foreign Minister Togo arrived at the Imperial Palace in the morning to meet with Emperor Hirohito. He gave the emperor a report on the bombing of Hiroshima. He told Hirohito that Japan should accept the Potsdam Declaration and end the war as soon as possible.

Japan's leader replied that, with this new weapon, "it had become even more impossible than ever to continue the war."

Togo left and met with Prime Minister Suzuki to set up a meeting with all of the emperor's advisors.

Dr. Michihiko Hachiya

Dr. Hachiya felt better this morning, though his body still hurt in several places. Dr. Katsube, one of the doctors who had treated him, came to visit. Hachiya asked when he could get up and start treating patients.

"You are too impatient," Katsube said. "You should be thankful that you are going to live."

Those words stunned Hachiya. "Was I that bad off?" he replied.

Katsube described how much blood he had lost. He said Hachiya would need to stay off his feet for a week.

During the day, some staff moved Hachiya to the second floor of the hospital, where the fire had been. Since the first floor was in better shape, it would be used for patients rather than the injured staff. The second floor had large windows that looked out over Hiroshima.

The bombing of Hiroshima left behind a haunting wasteland that stretched as far as the eye could see.

Now, for the first time, Hachiya could see how the bomb had destroyed most of the city. It was worse than anything he had ever seen. And he soon learned that some people on the edge of Hiroshima had a new word for the blast. They had seen a flash—or *pika*. That was followed by a loud boom—or *don*. The bombing of August 6 was now called the pika don.

Tsutomo Yamaguchi

Nagasaki, Japan,
August 8, 1945

Tsutomo Yamaguchi's train pulled into Nagasaki in the morning. His injured arm was swollen and getting worse. He knew he had to get to a doctor. Meanwhile, Japanese warplanes were patrolling the skies, keeping a watch for enemy bombers.

Yamaguchi went to the hospital and found an old classmate who was now a doctor there. The doctor drained the injured arm of pus and bandaged it. He gave Yamaguchi a white sheet to cover his burns and protect them from the sun. Then Yamaguchi went to his parents' house because his wife and son were staying at a new address, and he did not know its exact location.

Seeing him wrapped in the sheet and bandages, Mrs. Yamaguchi cried out, "Ghost!" Yamaguchi assured his mother he was not a ghost—he had survived the Hiroshima bombing.

His wife and son soon stopped by the house, and the three of them returned to their home. Neighbors who knew that Yamaguchi had been in Hiroshima came over to ask questions.

"If you are wearing white clothes, they will reflect the heat ray, but black clothes easily burn," Yamaguchi explained. "Flying glass is dangerous and will cause severe injuries. And if you see a flash in the sky, crouch down in a sturdy shelter."

By then other survivors, who had traveled with Yamaguchi from Hiroshima, were telling residents what they had seen. They and Yamaguchi could only hope they would not face the same kind of destruction in Nagasaki.

The Fat Man atomic bomb waited to be loaded into Bockscar, the B-29 bomber that carried it to Nagasaki, Japan.

FAT MAN FALLS

Corporal Abe Spitzer

Tinian island, Pacific Ocean,
August 8, 1945, 11 p.m.

Corporal Spitzer joined the men of the other flight crews for another briefing. A rumor he had heard the day before was true—the 393rd was going to drop another "gimmick" on Japan. This second atomic bomb was nicknamed "Fat Man." In the briefing, an intelligence officer explained that this one was even more powerful than Little Boy. As with the Hiroshima bombing, the first planes would observe the weather over the various targets, and three planes would fly together to drop the bomb. This time Spitzer would fly on a B-29 called Bockscar. It would be the one carrying the bomb.

The first target for the mission was Kokura, where the Japanese had several factories that made weapons. The backup target was Nagasaki. That city also had factories that supplied the military.

At 3:30 a.m. on August 9, Spitzer and the rest of his crew boarded Bockscar. Spitzer sat close to the bomb. He knew that if the plane crashed, they would all be dead. As the plane roared down the runway and did not take off,

Bockscar carried the Fat Man atomic bomb to Nagasaki, Japan.

he worried there was a problem. He began to sweat. Finally the B-29 was airborne.

Around 7 a.m., several hours into the flight, Major Sweeney told Spitzer, "Be ready for that weather report." If it was too cloudy over Kokura, the planes would head to Nagasaki. Then a report came in: "Weather good. Primary target recommended for bombing."

But as the B-29 approached Kokura, the weather worsened. Sweeney decided to head for Nagasaki.

Dr. Takashi Nagai

Nagasaki, Japan,
August 9, 1945, 10 a.m.

Just after 10 a.m., Dr. Nagai emerged from an air-raid shelter at his hospital. A U.S. plane had been spotted approaching the city, but then it had turned around. Nagai went back to work, which included preparing a lecture for one of his classes.

At 11:02 a.m., Nagai saw a flash of light outside his office window. *A bomb!* he thought. He wanted to dive down to take cover, but before he could, the window broke and pieces of glass flew into him, sending blood down his face. Objects in the room fell on him, and he could hear flames crackling nearby. With all the debris on top of him, he could not move. All he could do was cry for help.

Corporal Abe Spitzer

Above Nagasaki, Japan,
August 9, 1945, 11:02 a.m.

As Bockscar turned away from Nagasaki, Corporal Spitzer saw a flash of light. The blast from Fat Man seemed brighter than the one from Little Boy. Soon waves of energy rocked the plane, with one of them almost knocking him to the floor.

Looking out one of the plane's windows, Spitzer saw a rainbow of colors in the thick, black smoke. Everything seemed more intense than the first blast.

Fat Man's detonation laid waste to Nagasaki, Japan, with an explosive force equal to 21,000 tons of TNT.

Maybe that was not surprising, Spitzer reasoned, since Fat Man was more powerful than Little Boy.

Lieutenant Phil Barnes said, "I guess it's something we'll never forget."

"Don't worry," Spitzer said. "It'll stay with us, what we've just seen."

Soon after, Spitzer radioed his report back to the base at Tinian. Fat Man had been a success.

Tsutomo Yamaguchi

Nagasaki, Japan,
August 9, 1945

Tsutomo Yamaguchi woke with a fever, but he wanted to go to work anyway. People at his factory wanted to know what it had been like in Hiroshima. The questioners included his boss, who said, "I can't believe just one bomb destroyed the entire city."

As Yamaguchi heard those words, he saw a bright flash outside the office window. He knew right away it was from another bomb like the one that had flattened Hiroshima. He dove under a desk. In a few moments, he saw a mushroom cloud rise above the city—just like the one he had seen in Hiroshima.

His boss had taken cover too, and somehow both men survived the blast. Yamaguchi then headed home to check on his wife, Hisako, and their son. Their house was mostly destroyed, but Hisako and the boy were not there. Later, he found them in a bomb shelter near his factory. They were safe.

Seen from the ground, the atomic bomb blast over Nagasaki quickly swallowed the horizon with a monstrous cloud as the blast expanded outward.

Dr. Takashi Nagai

Nagasaki, Japan,
August 9, 1945

After a few moments, Dr. Nagai heard some of his staff outside the window. They managed to climb through the debris and get him out of the office. As he walked through the mostly ruined hospital, Nagai saw dead patients and staff everywhere. Some, who were still alive, called out, "I'm burning. Give me water. Pour water over me."

As fires approached the hospital, Nagai organized the staff to move patients to safer ground. Someone had bandaged the wound in his head from the glass, but it was still bleeding. A nurse took his pulse and realized he was in bad shape.

The nurse and some others forced the doctor to rest. It was not easy for him to sit, knowing some of the patients needed help. And looking out over the grounds, Nagai saw even more people streaming toward the hospital, hoping to get treatment for their wounds.

Survivors made their way down a road, carrying belongings and even each other, after the atomic bombing of Nagasaki.

Foreign Minister Shigenori Togo

Tokyo, Japan,
August 9, 1945, 2:30 p.m.

Foreign Minister Togo joined other ministers at the Imperial Palace. The day before, the Soviet Union had declared war on Japan. Soon after, Soviet forces had invaded Manchuria, a part of China that Japan had seized by military force in 1931.

Earlier that day, Togo had also learned about a second atomic bomb, this time dropped on Nagasaki. The first reports were that the damage was not as bad as in Hiroshima. But the blast weakened the argument of some of the generals who doubted the United States could drop more than one atomic bomb. No one in the Japanese government could say for sure now if another bomb might fall on another Japanese city.

Now Togo, once again, argued for peace with the Allies, following the outline of the Potsdam Declaration. But instead of an unconditional surrender, Togo insisted that the emperor be allowed to remain as ruler of Japan.

Not all of the other ministers present at this meeting agreed. General Korechika Anami and several others said there should be more conditions. They did not want Allied troops to occupy Japan. And they believed Japanese officials, not the Allies, should have the power to conduct any trials to see if anyone committed war crimes.

Togo doubted the Allies would accept all these conditions. But what would happen next was not up to him. Only the emperor could decide what Japan would do.

President Harry Truman

Washington, D. C.,
August 9, 1945, 10 p.m.

From the White House, President Truman spoke on the radio to the entire United States. He talked about the meeting he had just held in Potsdam and what the Allies would do to end the war. One of their major concerns was defeating Japan as quickly as possible.

Truman said, "The Japanese have seen what our atomic bomb can do. . . . If Japan does not surrender, bombs will have to be dropped on her war industries and, unfortunately, thousands of civilian lives will be lost. . . . We have used [the bomb] in order to shorten the agony of war, in order to save the lives of thousands and thousands of young Americans. . . . We shall continue to use it until we completely destroy Japan's power to make war. Only a Japanese surrender will stop us."

The president did not mention the dropping of the second atomic bomb on Nagasaki, though newspapers had already reported it. Truman knew that many people expected the war to end soon, in part because of the success of the two bombs.

Japanese Emperor Hirohito

A WAR ENDS, SUFFERING CONTINUES

7

Foreign Minister Togo again met with other top leaders of Japan. This time they were in a bomb shelter in the Imperial Palace. Rumors had spread that Tokyo could be the target of the next atomic bomb.

Emperor Hirohito entered the room, and for several hours he listened to his advisors say what he should do. Togo argued that Japan was suffering too much to make too many demands. The only demand they should insist upon was that the emperor remain in power.

As the discussion went on, some generals insisted that Japan should keep fighting, rather than seek any conditions. Finally, after several hours of talking, Prime Minister Suzuki looked at Hirohito. It was time for his decision.

Hirohito said, "I have the same opinion as the foreign minister. . . . We will risk losing everything if we continue a hopeless war. . . . I decide this way in order to save the people from disaster and to bring happiness to mankind around the world."

Tsutomo Yamaguchi

Nagasaki, Japan,
August 10, 1945

Together with his wife and son, Tsutomo Yamaguchi took shelter in a tunnel. His face and left arm were swelling more and turning purple. His arm had developed gangrene, an infection that kills healthy skin. Hisako was not sure how to treat her husband, but a stranger came by and offered to help. He gave Yamaguchi herbs to drink and sprinkled powder on his wounds. Slowly, he began to improve.

Dr. Takashi Nagai

Nagasaki, Japan,
August 10, 1945

Dr. Nagai and his staff woke up and saw the damage the fires had caused through the night. They went through the hospital and saw the charred remains of students, staff, and patients. Nagai had little faith that his wife, Midori, had survived the blast. If she were alive, she would have come to the hospital to look for him. But she had never come.

A nurse came up to him holding a pamphlet that had been dropped from a U.S. plane before the bombing. Nagai read the note, which told the citizens to leave Nagasaki as soon possible. The pamphlet said the United States had developed the most powerful weapon ever. Nagai's scientific training

U.S. bombers dropped thousands of leaflets, such as this one, warning Japanese citizens of the possible destruction of cities such as Hiroshima and Nagasaki.

convinced him that the weapon was an atomic bomb. He shared the note with Professor Seiki, a physicist who was nearby. The two men knew that Japan had also tried to build a bomb using uranium, but it had failed. And they knew one of the results of dropping an atomic bomb would be the release of huge amounts of radiation.

As the day went on, Nagai saw for himself the effects of the radiation. People who had no obvious injuries began falling to the ground. They were too

Only an arch remained of a Shinto shrine that was destroyed by the atomic blast that raced through Nagasaki.

weak to move. Nagai was starting to feel sick himself. But he knew that he would be ready the next day to try to help the people who were sicker than he was.

President Harry Truman

Washington, D. C.,
August 10, 1945, 12 p.m.

President Truman called a meeting of some of his top advisors to discuss a message that had just arrived from Japan. The Japanese were ready to talk about a surrender, if the emperor could remain as head of the nation.

Secretary of War Stimson believed the emperor should stay. He believed that many Japanese troops would not surrender if the emperor was removed. Secretary of State James Byrnes opposed this. He insisted that the Allies should stick to their demand for an unconditional surrender.

In the end, Truman accepted Stimson's argument. Later in the day, Truman met with more of his cabinet. He explained the Japanese offer and the U.S. response. Japan would keep the emperor in place, but the Allies would decide exactly what role he would play in a new Japanese government. And Truman made one more decision. He would stop dropping atomic bombs as the two sides tried to work out a peace deal. The president said the thought of wiping out another 100,000 people was too horrible. He was thinking especially of "all those kids."

Dr. Takashi Nagai

Nagasaki, Japan,
August 11, 1945

In the morning, Dr. Nagai and the staff continued to hunt for the wounded. Nagai stopped only when army doctors and nurses reached the area around the hospital. Now he felt free to go search for his wife. He wished he had searched for her sooner.

He entered their old neighborhood and saw ruined buildings everywhere. The radiation must be high, he thought, but he was determined to find Midori's body so he could give her a proper burial. Finding the spot where their house had stood, Nagai found all that was left of her—just some bones. He cried as he placed them in a bucket and then carried them to a nearby cemetery. He said out loud,

Dr. Takashi Nagai leaned on a pole as he searched the ruins in the Matsuyama District of Nagasaki just days after the atomic bombing.

"Forgive me for not going straight to you when you were dying. Please forgive me." He buried the bones and then returned to their home to see if anything had survived the blast and fires. He found some papers and some medals he had won while serving in the military. But then, weak from the radiation and lack of sleep and food, he collapsed.

President Harry Truman

Washington, D. C.,
August 14, 1945, 7 p.m.

As reporters gathered around him in the White House, President Truman prepared to read from a telegram he had received from the Swiss government. It contained a message from the Japanese ambassador in Switzerland. Japan was responding to a letter Secretary of State Byrnes had written regarding the Japanese offer for peace.

Truman read: "His Majesty the Emperor is prepared to authorize and ensure the signature of his Government and the Imperial General Headquarters of the necessary terms for carrying out the provisions of the Potsdam Declaration. His Majesty is also prepared to issue his commands to all the military, naval, and air authorities of Japan and all the forces under their control wherever located to cease active operations, to surrender arms and to issue such other orders as may be required by the Supreme Commander of the Allied Forces for the execution of the abovementioned terms."

At a press conference at the White House on August 14, 1945, President Harry Truman announced Japan's surrender.

After he finished talking, Truman and his wife, Bess, went out to the White House lawn. People were cheering and dancing, while car drivers honked their horns. Truman smiled as he watched the celebration. The American people knew the war was finally over.

Dr. Michihiko Hachiya

Hiroshima, Japan,
August 15, 1945, 12 p.m.

Dr. Hachiya gathered with others in an office building near the hospital. They were waiting to hear a radio broadcast from the government.

Over the past several days, Hachiya's strength had returned. He took a bicycle one day and rode through the streets, finally seeing for himself all the destruction. He rode by buildings that he knew and saw their remains. Back in the hospital, Hachiya was finally able to help take care of some of the wounded.

Now Hachiya stood in the back of the room and strained to hear the radio broadcast. He could not hear everything clearly, so he asked someone what the broadcast was about.

"The broadcast was in the emperor's own voice, and he has just said that we've lost the war," an official said.

Hachiya was stunned for two reasons. While leaders around the world often spoke on the radio, Emperor Hirohito had never done so before. But the doctor was especially stunned because of the emperor's message. Hachiya expected to hear that the government wanted the country to keep fighting, and he was ready to do so.

He went back to the hospital. People were crying, not believing that the war was over and Japan had lost. People began to cry out: "Only a coward would back out now!" and "I would rather die than be defeated!"

The idea of surrendering, Hachiya felt, was worse than what the atomic bomb had done to Hiroshima. But he realized that an order from the emperor could not be challenged. And he wondered what life would be like when the Americans came to Japan.

Representatives of Japan gathered on the deck of the USS *Missouri* in Tokyo Bay to sign a written agreement to officially surrender on September 2, 1945.

EPILOGUE

In the weeks after the emperor announced Japan's surrender, Dr. Takashi Nagai saw many more people sick from radiation. He became sick as well, though he managed to stay alive until 1951.

Other survivors of the Hiroshima and Nagasaki bombing were luckier. They lived much longer lives. Dr. Michihiko Hachiya recovered from his injuries. He continued to work as a doctor. After the war, he published a diary he had kept after the bombing of Hiroshima. Several years later, a U.S. doctor who met Hachiya learned about the diary and translated it into English. Published in 1955, the diary gave people in the United States a sense of what it was like for the Japanese after the atomic bombing.

Tsutomu Yamaguchi in 2006

Tsutomo Yamaguchi also recovered from his injuries and returned to his work as an engineer. Later in life, he began to speak out against the use of atomic weapons. So did Hideko Tamura. She came to the United States to study in 1952 and remained there. She married a U.S. citizen named Robert Snider and settled in Chicago. When she retired from her career as a social worker, Tamura Snider wrote and spoke often about the need for world peace.

At the end of the war, many of Japan's top government and military leaders were placed on trial for war crimes. They included Foreign Minister Shigenori Togo, who was found guilty and sentenced to 20 years in jail. He died in 1950.

For U.S. soldiers like Abe Spitzer and Bob Caron, the end of the war meant they could return to their families in the United States. Spitzer went home to New York and took a job in the garment industry. Caron used his skills in math and science to become an engineer.

After the war, Luis Alvarez continued working as a physicist. Much of his work was with cosmic rays—a form of energy that comes from far beyond Earth. In 1968 he received the Nobel Prize in Physics.

Luis Alvarez celebrated winning the Nobel Prize in 1968 with balloons decorated with the names of the subatomic particles that he and his team had discovered.

Harry Truman remained president of the United States until January 1953. By then the United States was at war again—this time in Korea. For most of Truman's time in office, U.S. troops occupied Japan. The country was forced to give up its military, though later it was allowed to rebuild it on a small scale. Emperor Hirohito served as a symbolic ruler of the country, as did the emperors after him. But real power was placed in an elected body called the National Diet, which was like the U.S. Congress. Japan is now a close ally of the United States.

Since 1945 various studies have tried to pinpoint how many people died in each city immediately when the bombs were dropped and soon after. By one estimate, at least 200,000 people died in Hiroshima and another 80,000 died in Nagasaki.

For a few years after the bombing of those two cities, the United States was the only country with atomic weapons. Since the 1950s the United States and several other countries have developed new radioactive explosives, called nuclear weapons, that are much more powerful than the two bombs dropped on Japan. The most powerful U.S. nuclear bomb is 80 times more destructive than the bomb dropped on Hiroshima.

Since 1945 no country has used a nuclear weapon during war. Many people in Japan and around the world have also called for limiting the number of nuclear weapons built or getting rid of them completely. They fear the massive destruction today's nuclear weapons would create.

Many historians have debated whether the United States should have dropped Little Boy and Fat Man in August 1945. Some say that the United States could have done a test bombing, as some scientists suggested at the time. Others say Japan was close to defeat anyway, especially with the Soviet Union entering the war. But defenders of President Truman's decision to use the bombs say he saved the lives of thousands of U.S. troops. The military was preparing to invade Japan, and losses could have been high. And intelligence reports showed that some Japanese military leaders were ready to keep fighting. The bombs seemed to convince Togo and others that the time had come for Japan to surrender.

Despite these debates, the facts are that Truman did order the use of these deadly new weapons. As people noted at the time, the world had entered a new era—when a single bomb could lay waste to an entire city.

TIMELINE

SEPTEMBER 1939: Germany invades Poland, starting World War II.

DECEMBER 7, 1941: Japan bombs Pearl Harbor in Hawaii, and the United States enters World War II.

1942: The United States and Great Britain start working together on the Manhattan Project to develop an atomic bomb.

FEBRUARY 1943: Major work on the atomic bomb begins in Los Alamos, New Mexico.

JULY 16, 1945: The United States tests the first atomic bomb at the Trinity site in New Mexico.

JULY 18, 1945: While attending a conference in Potsdam, Germany, President Harry Truman learns about the successful testing of the atomic bomb in New Mexico.

JULY 24, 1945: U.S. and British leaders decide to drop atomic bombs on Japan within the next few weeks.

AUGUST 6, 1945: A B-29 bomber named Enola Gay drops the first atomic bomb on Hiroshima, Japan, causing widespread death and destruction.

AUGUST 7, 1945: Japanese leaders meet to discuss surrendering to the Allies.

AUGUST 8, 1945: The Soviet Union declares war on Japan.

AUGUST 9, 1945: A B-29 bomber named Bockscar drops a second atomic bomb on the city of Nagasaki, Japan.

AUGUST 10, 1945: Japan's emperor, Hirohito, tells his advisors to seek peace with the Allies.

AUGUST 14, 1945: President Truman reads a message from the Japanese government indicating it is ready to surrender.

AUGUST 15, 1945: Emperor Hirohito speaks to the Japanese people and tells them about the surrender.

SEPTEMBER 2, 1945: Japanese and U.S. officials sign a peace treaty, officially ending World War II.

GLOSSARY

Allies (AL-lyz)—a group of countries including the United States, England, and France that fought together in World War II

ambassador (am-BA-suh-duhr)—a government official who represents his or her country

civilian (si-VIL-yuhn)—a person who is not in the military

debris (duh-BREE)—remains of something broken or destroyed

detonator (DET-uh-nate-uhr)—a device that makes bombs explode

diplomat (DIP-lo-mat)—a representative of a government who handles his or her country's foreign relations

intelligence (in-TEL-uh-jenss)—information about an enemy's plans or actions

obliterate (oh-BLIT-uh-rate)—to destroy something completely

pamphlet (PAM-flit)—a printed publication without a hard cover

physicist (FIZ-uh-sist)—a scientist who studies matter and energy

radiation (ray-dee-AY-shuhn)—a form of energy that in small doses has medical uses, but can cause illness or death in large doses

shell (SHELL)—an explosive fired from large military guns

Soviet Union (SOH-vee-et YOON-yuhn)—a former federation of 15 republics that included Russia, Ukraine, and other nations of eastern Europe and northern Asia; also called the Union of Soviet Socialist Republics (USSR)

TNT (TNT)—an explosive commonly used in military weapons

turret (TUR-it)—an enclosed part of an airplane that holds a gun

CRITICAL THINKING QUESTIONS

1. President Truman's advisors had different opinions about how the atomic bombs should be used against Japan. Some thought they should be dropped in remote areas. Others felt cities with weapons plants should be targeted. Why do you think Truman ultimately decided to drop the bombs on Hiroshima and Nagasaki? Do you think it was the right decision? Explain why or why not.

2. The United States bombed Nagasaki just three days after Hiroshima. Was that enough time for the Japanese government to decide whether or not to continue fighting the war? Would they have surrendered without Nagasaki being bombed as well? Explain your answers.

3. The bombings of Hiroshima and Nagasaki brought the world into the nuclear age. Since then several other countries, including the United States and Russia, have built up large nuclear weapons arsenals. But since 1945, no country has used nuclear weapons in war again. Why do you think that is the case?

INTERNET SITES

Atomic Bomb Museum
http://atomicbombmuseum.org

Hiroshima Peace Memorial Museum
http://hpmmuseum.jp

Manhattan Project National Historical Park
https://www.nps.gov/mapr

World War II in the Pacific
https://www.nationalgeographic.org/interactive/world-war-ii-pacific

FURTHER READING

Blake, Kevin. *Harry S. Truman: The 33rd President*. A First Look at America's Presidents. New York: Bearport Publishing, 2016.

Doeden, Matt. *The Manhattan Project*. Heroes of World War II. Minneapolis: Lerner Publications, 2019.

Duling, Kaitlyn. *The Order to Drop the Atomic Bomb, 1945*. America's Most Important Documents: Inquiry into Historical Sources. New York: Cavendish Square, 2019.

Langley, Andrew. *Hiroshima and Nagasaki*. Eyewitness to World War II. North Mankato, MN: Compass Point Books, 2017.

Roesler, Jill. *Eyewitness to the Dropping of the Atomic Bombs*. Eyewitness to World War II. Mankato, MN: Child's World, 2016.

SELECT BIBLIOGRAPHY

Alvarez, Luis. *Adventures of a Physicist*. New York: Basic Books, 1987.

Caron, George R., and Charlotte E. Meares. *Fire of a Thousand Suns: The George R. "Bob" Caron Story, Tail Gunner of the Enola Gay*. Westminster, CO: Web Publishing, 1995.

Frank, Richard B. *Downfall: The End of the Imperial Japanese Empire*. New York: Penguin Books, 1999.

Glynn, Paul. *A Song for Nagasaki: The Story of Takashi Nagai—Scientist, Convert, and Survivor of the Atomic Bomb*. San Francisco: Ignatius Press, 2009.

Hachiya, Michihiko. *Hiroshima Diary: The Journal of a Japanese Physician, August 6–September 30, 1945*. Edited and translated by Warner Wells. Chapel Hill, NC: University of North Carolina Press, 1995.

Hersey, John. *Hiroshima*. New York: Alfred A. Knopf, 2005.

Kurzman, Dan. *Day of the Bomb: Countdown to Hiroshima*. New York: McGraw-Hill, 1986.

McCullough, David. *Truman*. New York: Simon and Schuster, 1992.

Pellegrino, Charles. *The Last Train from Hiroshima: The Survivors Look Back*. New York: Henry Holt, 2010.

Snider, Hideko Tamura. *One Sunny Day: A Child's Memories of Hiroshima*. Chicago: Open Court, 1996.

Southard, Susan. *Nagasaki: Life after Nuclear War*. New York: Penguin Books, 2015.

Spitzer, Abe, and Merle Miller. *We Dropped the Atom Bomb*. N.p.: CreateSpace Independent Publishing Platform, 2016.

Weller, George. First into Nagasaki: *The Censored Eyewitness Dispatches on Post-Atomic Japan and Its Prisoners of War*. Edited by Anthony Weller. New York: Crown Publishers, 2006.

INDEX

ABOUT THE AUTHOR

Michael Burgan is a freelance writer who specializes in books for children and young adults, both fiction and nonfiction. A graduate of the University of Connecticut with a degree in history, Burgan is also a produced playwright and the editor of *The Biographer's Craft*, the newsletter for Biographers International Organization. He lives in Santa Fe, New Mexico.